ANDREW LINES

PHOENIX RISING

THE RITE JOURNEY

MAN MADE

PHOENIX RISING

A MAN MADE RITE JOURNEY

BY ANDREW LINES

This book presents a process by which we, as parents, carers and mentors, can help children in our care to grow and develop in their passage from children to adults.

Throughout, the author suggests a variety of learnings, experiences and events that might be a part of developing a responsible, resilient, resourceful and respectful young adult. Often, these recommendations are drawn from the author's own experiences.

While this book makes a range of suggestions and recommendations, as every child is different, it is essential that parents and carers consider, decide and take responsibility for which experiences, opportunities and discussions are appropriate for the child or children in our care.

In these circumstances, Authenticity Pty Ltd and the author accept no liability for the suggestions and recommendations in this book or for any outcomes flowing from adoption of those suggestions or recommendations.

PREFACE

On the 5th of June, 2017, my youngest son Phoenix and I set off on an adventure. A trip that would see him leave a boy but return a beginning young man.

I had taken my elder son, Malachi, on a similar trip in March 2014. We headed to Central Australia where I had planned to take him through his Rite Journey, a Rite of Passage (RoP) process, to initiate him into young adulthood.

For many years I had been facilitating Rites of Passage in the school setting, however, neither of my own sons were attending a Rite Journey school and so I decided to facilitate their own Rite Journey RoP process.

Using the hallmarks of our Rite Journey program, conversations which cover important topics about stepping into adulthood and the seven stages of The Hero's Journey, I created an experience for my sons.

What follows is an account of the trip I made with Phoenix.

The content was originally written as a series of Facebook posts and I have retained the nature of these, whilst in some sections adding some more detail for clarification.

Whilst the trip I made was overseas and for a number of weeks, it is possible to create a similar process over a shorter period of time and closer to home.

I hope that you might find some inspiration in the pages that follow for creating a Rite of Passage for the boy or girl in your life.

PART 1

As the cycle of life would have it, the day that we begin to celebrate and honour Phoenix's transition from boyhood to manhood we also honoured the passing of dear Granny.

This afternoon we held a little ceremony at home to remember Inge who became affectionately known as 'Yoghurt Granny'. We planted a Granny Smith tree in the yard, remembering her own apple tree in her yard in Leicester, England, and her love of stewed apples.

'Yoghurt Granny'

We now have a place to reflect on her courage and determination, given that she fled East Germany to find a better life in the UK for her and her baby boy.

This evening we met together as a family to begin celebrating Phoenix's journey - **The Departure**.

The process began by reflecting on his birth and his childhood, taking him back to his early years and what better way to do that than surrounded by loving family including, siblings, step-siblings, grandparents, aunt, uncle and cousins?

We pinned up photos of him as a young child. We spoke of his cheeky smile, his love of life and his sense of fun.

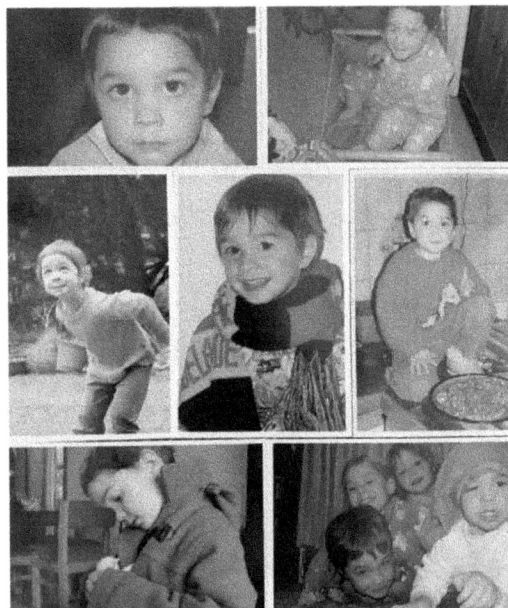

Phoenix - his early years

On the eve of our trip away Phoenix and I have chosen to stay at Nanna and Grandad's.

Phoenix's day finished by being taken back to his pre-school years when Nanna would visit on Thursday evenings, bring her world famous pasties for dinner and then read him a story as he went to bed.

Tonight we reflected on those special boyhood times as Nanna wound back the clock and read one of his favourite books from back when he was a boy, 'Are we there yet?' by Alison Lester, an apt title given what awaits us at 4am tomorrow.

But that is a story for another day.

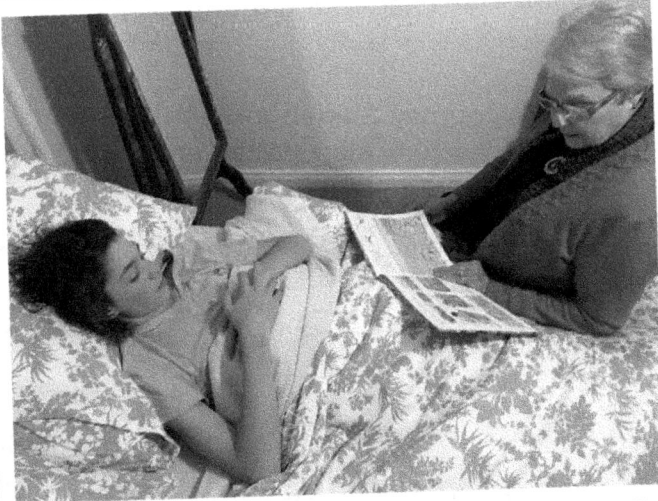

Phoenix reminiscing with Nanna

PART 2

The next few weeks will include plenty of conversations about being a good, strong man and as Phoenie's guide/mentor on his journey I will be looking for opportunities to initiate such chats.

Today as we travelled to the airport we were blessed with a cab driver who had chosen a less common life path of travel including living and working in many different countries in his life.

He had decided to focus his life on travel rather than work. His story was a perfect example of the variety of options we have to choose from in life.

And then at the airport we bought the morning paper and had a conversation about the shocking news from London, the way some men choose to create terror and others choose to be heroes.

Grabbing the moment to chat about what is current, relevant and applicable to life as a man is what this journey will be all about.

We'll also use our **Rite Journey Guidebook** along the way to guide our conversations as well as the **Man Made Cards**.

The journey begins...

The Advertiser

ENGLAND'S TERROR BLITZ
Seven killed as maniacs mow down pedestrians and stab pub-goers in third outrage in 10 weeks

KNIFE TO LONDON'S HEART

PART 3

As I mentioned earlier, I completed a similar RoP process with my elder son Malachi back in 2014.

For that journey we headed to Central Australia, however for Phoenix we are travelling a little further afield.

Stage one of the flight took us to Hong Kong and we watched the movie Hacksaw Ridge and had a great discussion around war, faith, selflessness and sacrifice. It's a powerful story.

Once landed in Hong Kong we chatted about the traditional male initiation and Rites of Passage from around the world.

We looked at Indigenous Aboriginal Rites, South American Bullet Ant Gloves and the platform diving in Vanuatu.

(You can check that out **here** - "Just before diving the boys say their most intimate thoughts. They could be their last.")

Hacksaw Ridge

Traditional male initiation

Phoenix also created a personal symbol, about the things that are important in his life, and I shared mine with his.

The Following stage of The Rite Journey is related to having mentors throughout life who are both role models and people available for advice and direction. Prior to leaving on our trip I asked a dozen influential men in Phoenix's life to handwrite him a letter of welcome to manhood. I did this without Phoenix's knowledge and over the course of his journey I would pass on one of these letters every now and then. In Hong Kong, I surprised Phoenix with two of these handwritten letters...from his grandfathers, Barry and Roger.

In his journal Phoenix distilled the essence of what his grandpas were letting him know about being a man and also the qualities that he sees in them that he would like to replicate as a man.

I have kept these letters private between Phoenix and his grandfathers but I do love watching his face as he reads them and contemplates the importance of these good, strong men in his life.

Personal symbols

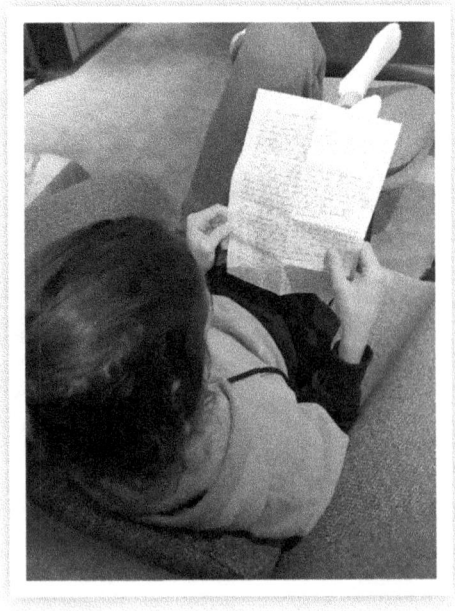

Phoenix reading his letters

PART 3.5

A brief post today...we have literally just arrived, very late evening, at our first port of call. Here's Phoenix's first look at NYC.

PART 4

Today we stepped out of our room early and ventured for Phoenix's first real daytime look at NYC.

Today Phoenix began his day by grabbing a NYC brekky of a Bagel and croissant and then we ventured to Fed Ex to print off our entry ticket for the Empire State Building. In the Fed Ex store there were two books for sale, yes, just the two. And one of them was a very favourite Dr Seuss book of mine

9

I love the serendipity that I observe in life and this was one of those moments. What better book could I have stumbled upon with Phoenix, on his Rite Journey than "Oh, the places you'll go".

I read it to him right there in the Fed Ex store, bought him a copy and we chatted about its various messages (including following your path, learning lessons and bouncing back from the down times) as we wandered towards one of the places Phoenix had always wanted to see - The Empire State Building.

Here we met one of the few New Yorkers I know, Carol, and she happens to work in the ESB so was able to help us get to the top and also show us her office with a view!!!

We marvelled at the feat of construction, the dedication of the workmen, not to mention their ability to deal with heights (not a strength of Phoenix's or mine).

We also spent the time with a couple of Carol's Californian friends and it was lovely seeing Phoenix's face light up as he had the opportunity to explain to a couple of Americans all about Aussie Rules footy. He couldn't believe they knew nothing!

Our FedEx store discovery!

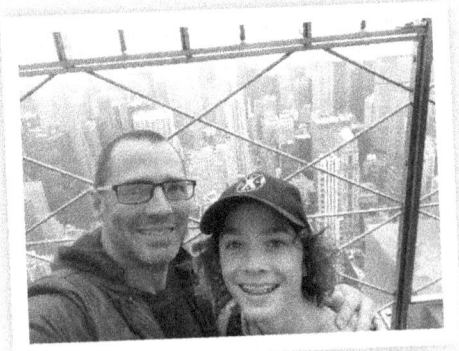

The view from the ESB

We then hopped on a tour bus and headed for lunch in Little Italy where we dined on delicious pizza and Phoenix read letters from his three uncles.

Then a trip to Chinatown for Phoenix to find a new phone cover (he is a 15 yo after all) and then we returned to our accommodation for a nap (I am in my 40s after all).

Having napped, we headed out to another special request of Phoenix's, to see a baseball game... so we went to Yankee Stadium to see the NY Yankees play the Boston Red Sox (for the record the Yankees lost 4-5).

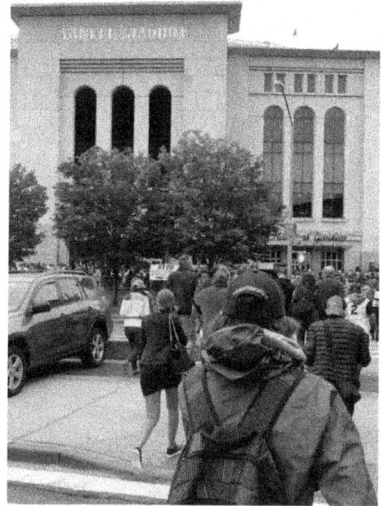

On our way to Yankee Stadium

The atmosphere was amazing and we had the opportunity to talk about our shared love of sport and my choice to invest over the years in supporting this love by purchasing season tickets to my beloved Adelaide Crows and also having membership at Adelaide Oval for cricket games too. I told Phoenix that investing in my passions is something that has been a real positive for my mental health.

As we travelled on the subway back to see the view from the Empire State Building at night we had rich conversations based on the **'My Stuff' suit** from the **Man Made Cards**.

We chatted about a whole variety of things about Phoenix, who he is and how he feels about himself. The Man Made Cards are a great vehicle for getting such sharing happening.

After the night visit to ESB we wandered through Times Square and headed back to our accommodation by 1.30am.

Today was filled with wonder and awe as we shared the sights of NYC together, but what also made it extra special was the conversations which were authentic and abundant.

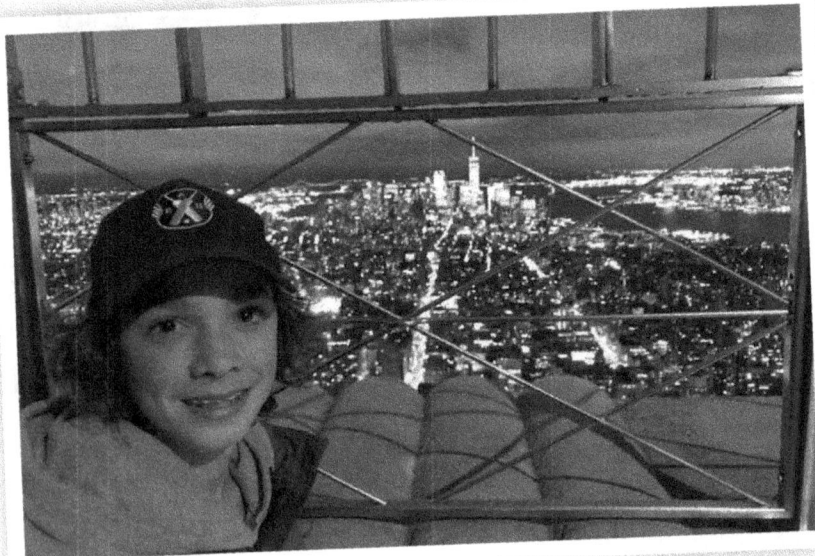

Our night visit to the Empire State Building

PART 5

There were a few things I wanted to focus on for today's experience in NYC and they largely had to do with being in this amazing city as well as a couple of important elements regarding being a gentleman.

Firstly I let Phoenix know that he was in charge of navigation and where we went for the day.

I wanted him to take responsibility for getting us around this big city, learning to use the subway and getting a feel for the lay out of NYC.

We have a Metro Pass and I encouraged him to be bold, chatting about "What's the worst that can happen? We just hop back on another train in the other direction!"

I had some plans but knew that we would probably stumble across the places I wanted to go to, so we left our AirBNB at 10.30 with Phoenix deciding we'd hop on the subway and head down to 34th Street.

Our assistant, Amauri

I initiated a chat about finding your style as a man. What it is about choosing to look good, smell good and feel good about yourself and how you are in the world. And what better place to explore that than in one of the style capitals of the world.

Our first stop was Macy's where I took Phoenix to the men's fragrance section and explained that we were here to learn about smelling good! I asked him to have a look at and choose the assistant who he thought would be the person for the job and he chose Amauri.

Phoenix exploring the men's fragrance section

Amauri took us through the details of various fragrances, citrus, floral, spicy, woody, what might be best for day, for night, what might be best for summer, for winter and why. He also explained the difference between eau de parfum and eau de toilette.

Phoenix sampled fragrances from Tom Ford, Bulgari, Mont Blanc and Polo.

It was such a wonderful experience for him and great to see how the assistants helped him understand the world of fragrance.

From there we moved onto chatting about fashion and style.

Phoenix, being a sports lover, had saved up to buy a pair of sports shoes from NYC and so we scoured the footwear shops and eventually found THE shoes in the 5th Avenue Flagship Adidas store.

The Dame 3s were his choice and a good choice too!

But style is not all about the right sports shoe and so we moved on to the corner of East 44th and Madison where I spied a men's clothing store out of the corner of my eye.

Phoenix with his brand new 'Dame 3s'

I stopped Phoenie and suggested we pop into the clothing store for a minute to see if someone could chat to him about dressing well, and boy, we hit the jackpot. Serendipity again!

I had no idea that we had just walked into Brooks Brothers, the clothing store which has dressed all but 5 of the American Presidents.

We had Ricky take us under his wing and he spent the next 80 minutes with us. He explained to Phoenix everything about looking good from shoes matching your belt to the importance of pocket squares in 'lifting' a suit jacket.

Phoenix spent 15 minutes learning how to tie a bow tie. He also heard about which suits to wear for different occasions, lapel thicknesses, tuxedos, classic suits, modern suits, sports coats and collar styles.

We heard how the company is 199 years old, how Abraham Lincoln was inaugurated and assassinated in a Brooks Brothers suit. We looked in the mirror that Abe used to check his suits and met Mario who dresses Donald Trump.

It was such a memorable time for both of us and another opportunity to chat with Phoenix about serendipity and the generosity of people.

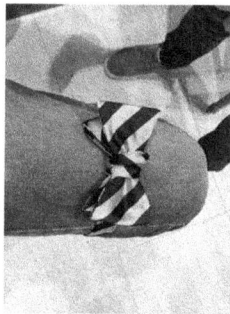

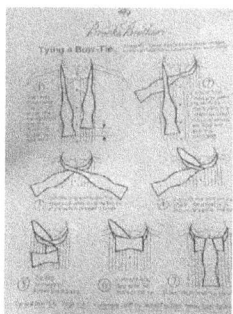

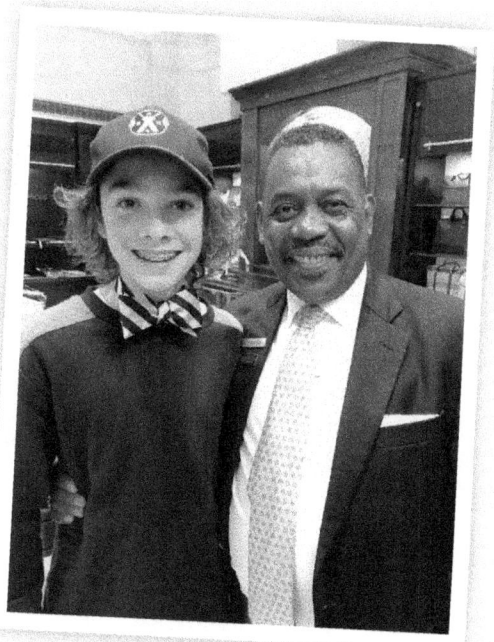

Phoenix being shown the ropes by Ricky in Brooks Brothers

Ricky shared about serving Janet Jackson (he has a book filled with messages from his customers over the last 15 years), his upbringing in North Carolina where he couldn't mix with the white kids and his love for his children and grandchildren. We sure were blessed with his help.

Phoenix decided that our next stop would be the 9/11 Memorial, a powerful and sobering reflection on an event which occurred almost exactly 6 months to the day before Phoenix's birth.

There was very little conversation throughout the visit, the enormity of the event and the experience of those who were affected and those who were heroes was overwhelming.

The 9/11 Memorial

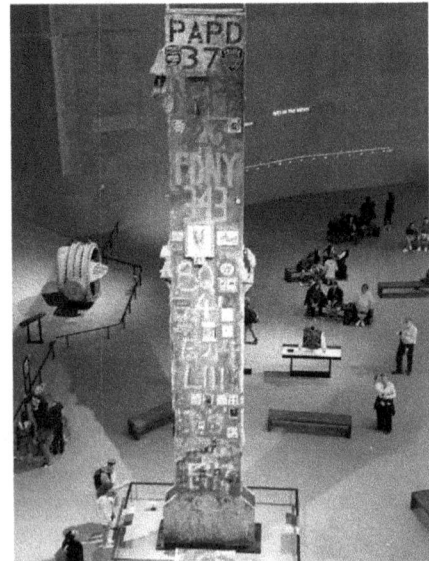

Finally we caught up for dinner with one of my mentors, Miles Groth, Professor of Psychology at Wagner College on Staten Island. Miles was probably the first major supporter of me and The Rite Journey. I met him in Adelaide back in 2006 and he encouraged me to continue developing TRJ and invited me to NYC back in 2008 to share my work.

It was such a pleasure to introduce Phoenix to Miles and to have Miles share his story with Phoenix... a story of staying positive whatever life throws at you and following your own dream rather than what others dream for you!

Another full and memorable day with plenty for Phoenix to consider.

You will be noticing the variety of kinds of experiences and conversations that can be used as a part of a RoP experience. Some of these moments have been carefully planned but others are very much more spur of the moment, serendipitous chats.

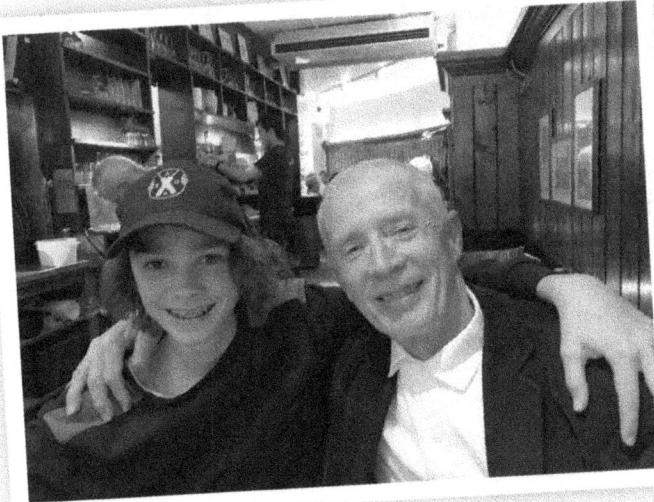

Phoenix with one of my own
mentors, Miles Groth

PART 6

One of the important elements of creating conversations in a contemporary Rite of Passage process, be it in the classroom with The Rite Journey or on the trips with my boys, has been the flexibility to be open to noticing the right time to have certain conversations.

I have an idea of the conversations and topics I'd like to cover throughout the duration of the trip. On occasions I will know that I want to discuss a particular topic at a particular place but at other times an opportunity might arise and I will choose to take it.

I'm appreciating having the **Man Made Cards** (something that I hadn't made when I took Malachi away).

I designed the cards following a workshop on creating a RoP that I ran after Malachi's trip.

A couple of the guys at the workshop said to me 'It's OK for you Andrew, you've been doing this stuff for years and you know the conversations to have with boys but what about us?"

Hence, I created the Man Made Cards, a set of 87 cards containing 412 questions divided into 6 suits. It came in handy today.

We had decided that today would be a bus tour through Harlem, a couple of museum visits and I was looking forward to sharing my love of Seinfeld with Phoenix during the day. Other than that I would see what might unfold.

We strolled out of our accommodation on 108th West and headed Northwest to Broadway as I wanted to show Phoenie the legendary Tom's Restaurant, a famous Seinfeld landmark.

Following that we wandered to the Cathedral of Saint John the Divine. We went inside for a peek and then I had a brief chat with Phoenix about faith and religion. We then waited at our bus stop for the tour bus which we thought might be minutes away but before too long it became clear that we might be waiting for a while. So this was one of those opportunities where I thought we could have a bit of a chat... so I opened up the **Man Made Cards**, found the **Big Stuff Suit** and we explored those topics for 20-30 minutes sitting on the steps of the Cathedral.

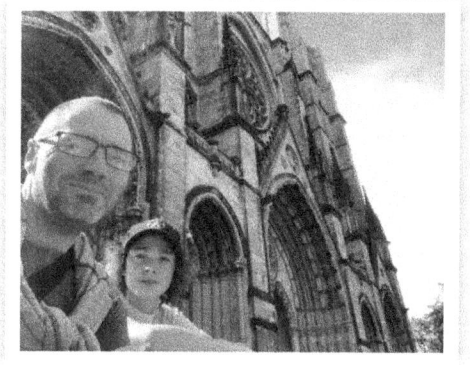

Finally the bus arrived and we travelled through Harlem and then ended up at the Museum of the City of New York where we learned about the history of the city from its original settlement. We chatted about the significant faith it took for people arriving to start their new lives in NYC.

From here we visited the Metropolitan Museum of Art. We saw an amazing array of wonderful art from ancient Roman and Greek sculptures, to European classics and modern American Art. We chatted about the significance of art in history.

We also had one of those moments where we stumbled across a conversation point. In the Oceana section we discovered a series of artifacts from the initiation of boys.

We chatted about the processes of male initiation which include the mother energy and the separation from it that often happens in initiation.

Check out the photo of the process the boys go through with the female figure (Tetekepu).

We noted the common use of masks in initiation, either instilling an element of fear in the initiates or using them to scare off the women, children and uninitiated men from the ceremony.

From The Met we ambled through Central Park to the American Museum of Natural History (site of the movie 'Night at the Museum'). Another serendipitous moment as we line up for tickets and Phoenix said "Dad, check out that quote." I looked up to see a quote titled 'Manhood' by Theodore Roosevelt, it's a beauty.

Female Figure (Tetepeku)
Abelam people, Prince Alexander Mountains, Sepik region, Papua New Guinea, 19th or early 20th century
Wood, paint

MANHOOD

A MANS USEFULNESS DEPENDS
UPON HIS LIVING UP TO HIS IDEALS
INSOFAR AS HE CAN
IT IS HARD TO FAIL BUT IT
IS WORSE NEVER TO HAVE TRIED
TO SUCCEED
ALL DARING AND COURAGE
ALL IRON ENDURANCE OF MISFORTUNE
MAKE FOR A FINER NOBLER TYPE
OF MANHOOD
ONLY THOSE ARE FIT TO LIVE
WHO DO NOT FEAR TO DIE AND NONE
ARE FIT TO DIE WHO HAVE SHRUNK
FROM THE JOY OF LIFE AND THE
DUTY OF LIFE   THEODORE ROOSEVELT

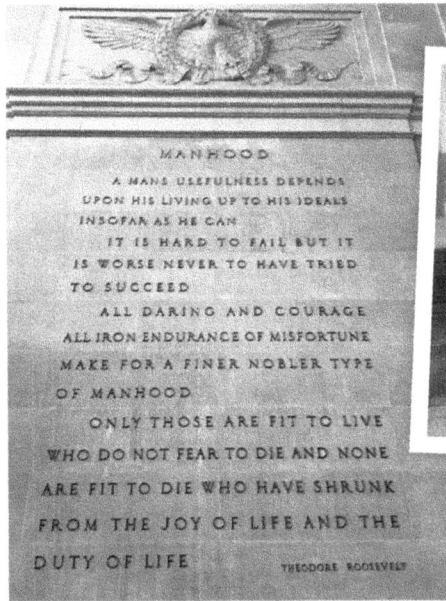

Above left
Mask
Probably Nissan Island, northern Solomon Islands, late 19th–early 20th century
Bark cloth, wood, bamboo, paint

Inside we discovered more historical initiation rituals from West Africa and the Congo...

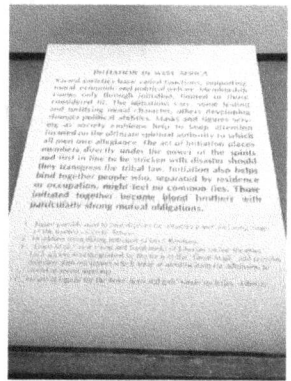

ENTRY INTO ADULT LIFE

Some dances pertain only to initiation rites introducing children to adult responsibilities. In the region of Liberia the Poro and Sande initiation societies aim to prepare both boys and girls for a worthy adult life. Costumes with frightening aspect symbolize for the children the wrath and power of ancestral spirits who watch over their descendants and punish transgression. The children also learn respect and reverence, for life is not ruled by fear alone. The dances and costumes often reflect totemic belief, certain animals or birds symbolizing aspects of spiritual existence. Such costumes usually cover the whole body, even fingers and toes. Sometimes dancers become lax and take less care to clothe themselves correctly. Any subsequent illness is broken with the be charged directly to this relaxation and tradition restored to its original purity by appropriate ritual.

Dinner was a spontaneous catch up with one of my NYC friends, Kyle and his fiancé Joanna, sushi just off of Broadway and then we had one of our treats for the trip, watching Jerry Seinfeld live at the Beacon Theater. A delightful and amusing end to another full day of father/son adventures and conversation. I am just loving the uninterrupted time we are getting to spend together.

Jerry Seinfeld live at the Beacon Theater

PART 7

Today is our last day in NYC, we fly out at 7.30pm. I had left it to Phoenix to decide what he'd like to see before we flew out. He was keen to visit Top of the Rock (Rockefeller Building) and to see the Statue of Liberty, so that was the plan.

As far as conversations for the day went I knew that I wanted to show Phoenix John D Rockefeller's "I believe" plaque in the Rockefeller Plaza. When I was last in NYC, 10 years ago, reading his statement had a real impact on me.

So I wondered if the day might be about personal values and wisdom to live by.

And as the day panned out there were a few moments that serendipitously appeared.

As we were leaving our accommodation and farewelling our host I saw a book in the bookcase titled 'Daily Rituals'. I asked if I could have a quick look and our host explained that it was a book about successful people's various daily rituals.

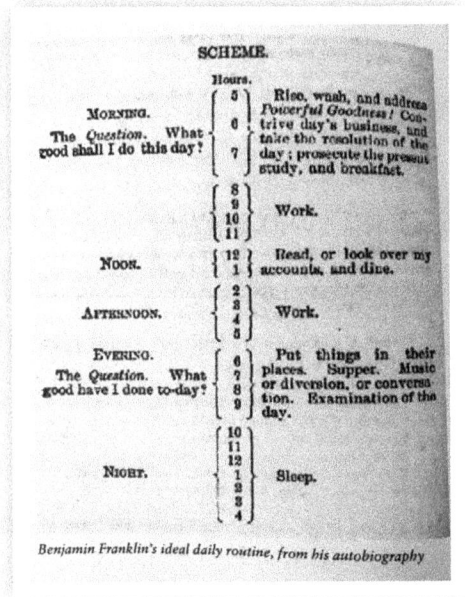

Benjamin Franklin's ideal daily routine, from his autobiography

Benjamin Franklin's daily routine

The first of these in the book was Benjamin Franklin's ideal daily routine (see photo). What struck me was his morning question and his evening question.

Morning - "What good shall I do this day?"
Evening - "What good have I done today?"

Phoenix and I chatted about how beginning your day with such a question is a great way of setting a positive intention and looking outside of yourself. We chatted about one of the shifts from 'child psychology' to 'adult psychology' being a move from 'life is about me' to 'life is about others'.

The second moment was on board our subway train B as we headed downtown. A girl directly across from us was reading 'The Alchemist' by Paulo Coehlo.

I was reminded of my love for the book and that in recent years I have bought a copy of it, as a graduation gift, for my students upon finishing year 12. I pointed it out to Phoenix and let him know of the significance the book had held in my life and made a mental note to see if I could find a copy of it sometime during the day!

Fortunately, the airport bookshop had the exact same edition that the girl was reading. Brilliant! So I purchased that at the end of the day and gave it to Phoenie.

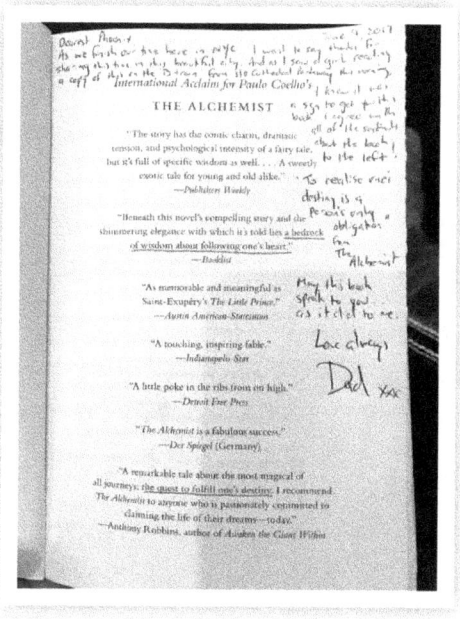

At the Rockefeller Plaza I asked Phoenix to read the "I believe" plaque and then I reread it to him, making sure he got the gist of each of the statements. They are such powerful words and ones that I will continue to hold dear.

"I believe in the supreme worth of the individual and in his right to life, liberty and the pursuit of happiness.

I believe that every right implies a responsibility, every opportunity, an obligation; every possession a duty.

I believe that the law was made for man and not man for the law; that government is the servant of the people and not their master.

I believe in the dignity of labor, whether with head or hand; that the world owes no man a living but it owes every man an opportunity to make a living.

I believe that thrift is essential to well-ordered living and that economy is a prime request of a sound financial structure, whether in government, business or personal affairs.

I believe in the sacredness of a promise, that a man's word should be as good as his bond; that character - not wealth or power or position - is of supreme worth.

I believe that the rendering of useful service is the common duty of mankind and that only in the purifying fire of sacrifice is the dross (waste matter) of selfishness consumed and the greatness of the human soul set free.

I believe in all-wise and all-loving God, named by whatever name, and that the individuals highest fulfillment, greatest happiness, and widest usefulness are to be found in living in harmony with His will.

I believe that love is the greatest thing in the world; that it alone can overcome hate; that right can and will triumph over might."

John D. Rockefeller

Following this we had the opportunity to look out over the city again on a beautiful clear day and then headed out on a boat to the Statue of Liberty. We heard about the history of the statue and could discuss the concept of freedom and what was behind the gift of the statue from the French.

Finally, to finish the day I shared with Phoenix some of the important 'wisdom statements' that have been significant in my life. These included Goethe's verse on commitment, Miguel Ruiz's Four Agreements and a saying that they share with young men in the Native American initiation process.

I was so pleased with the way our day ended up becoming about wisdom. As Goethe says, when we're committed to a task "all sorts of things occur to help (us) that would never otherwise have occurred."

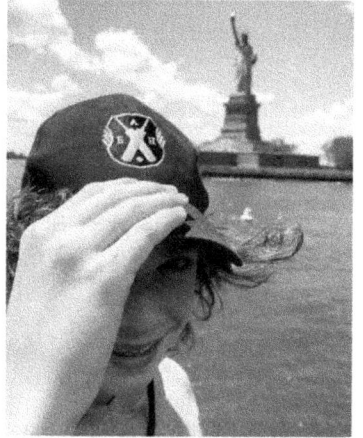

THE POWER OF COMMITMENT!

"UNTIL ONE IS COMMITTED, THERE IS HESITANCY, THE CHANCE TO DRAW BACK, ALWAYS INEFFECTIVE- NESS. CONCERNING ALL ACTS OF INITIATIVE (AND CREATION), THERE IS ONE ELEMENTARY TRUTH THE IGNORANCE OF WHICH KILLS COUNTLESS IDEAS AND SPLENDID PLANS: THAT THE MOMENT ONE DEF- INITELY COMMITS ONESELF, THEN PROVIDENCE MOVES TOO. ALL SORTS OF THINGS OCCUR TO HELP ONE THAT WOULD NEVER OTHERWISE HAVE OC- CURRED. A WHOLE STREAM OF EVENTS ISSUES FROM THE DECISION, RAISING IN ONE'S FAVOUR ALL MANNER OF UNFORESEEN INCIDENTS AND MEET- INGS AND MATERIAL ASSISTANCE, WHICH NO MAN COULD HAVE DREAMED WOULD HAVE COME HIS WAY.

WHATEVER YOU CAN DO OR DREAM YOU CAN, BEGIN IT. BOLDNESS HAS GENIUS, POWER AND MAGIC IN IT. BEGIN IT NOW".

—J. W. VON GOETHE

"A bit of advice Given to a young Native American At the time of his initiation:

As you go the way of life, You will see a great chasm. Jump. It is not as wide as you think."

Joseph Campbell

theritejourney.com

THE FOUR AGREEMENTS

1. BE IMPECCABLE WITH YOUR WORD
Speak with integrity. Say only what you mean. Avoid using the word to speak against yourself or to gossip about others. Use the power of your word in the direction of truth and love.

2. DON'T TAKE ANYTHING PERSONALLY
Nothing others do is because of you. What others say and do is a projection of their own reality, their own dream. When you are immune to the opinions and actions of others, you won't be the victim of needless suffering.

3. DON'T MAKE ASSUMPTIONS
Find the courage to ask questions and to express what you really want. Communicate with others as clearly as you can to avoid misunderstandings, sadness and drama. With just this one agreement, you can completely transform your life.

4. ALWAYS DO YOUR BEST
Your best is going to change from moment to moment; it will be different when you are healthy as opposed to sick. Under any circumstance, simply do your best, and you will avoid self-judgment, self-abuse and regret.

— MIGUEL RUIZ

PART 8

Yesterday we landed in Paris from NYC and I had a special spot I wanted to take Phoenix. We hired our car and drove North to Pozières, a village that was completely destroyed in World War I during what became the Battle of Pozières (23 July–7 August 1916), part of the Battle of the Somme. It is a hugely significant site in Australian history and I wanted the opportunity for Phoenix to experience visiting the site and for us to have some conversation about war and sacrifice.

Phoenix spied red poppies in the fields on the approach and we lunched at Tommy's, a well known local eating place for Aussies and then went and paid our respects and had a minute's silence at the 'site of the windmill' as well as visiting the Gibraltar Bunker and the memorial to the Australian 1st Division.

Today the site of the windmill the Germans had concreted into their strongpoint is inscribed with Bean's words: "The ruin of the Pozières Windmill which lies here was the centre of the struggle on this part of the Somme battlefield in July and August 1916. It was captured on August 4th by Australian troops who fell more thickly on this ridge than on any other battlefield of the war." Pozières, Bean wrote that this battlefield, "is more deeply sown with Australian sacrifice than any other place on earth."

In just six weeks at Pozières, Australia suffered 23,000 casualties, including 6800 deaths.

From there we headed to Bruges for a stroll through the beautiful, historic city and then headed for Ghent.

On our road trip I took control of the music in the car for an hour and took Phoenix through the evolution of my love of music. He heard about my favourite songs from when I was 8 (Computer Games) through to my love of a heap of bands over 40 years including Icehouse, Midnight Oil, U2, Ozzy, Megadeth and Dream Theater. I played an influential song from each band and then we discussed his musical preferences. Clearly not that influenced by mine. ;-)

The historical city of Bruges

Our riverboat home in Ghent

We arrived in Belgium, the home of waffles, beer, chocolate and The Rite Journey Europe! Another bit of serendipity on this trip was that today, June 11, is Father's Day in Belgium! So I had the opportunity to partake in one of my favourite Father's Days rituals... asking my kids the following questions. What am I doing well as a dad? What could I be doing better as a dad?

It was a lovely chat with Phoenix in the market square of Ghent.

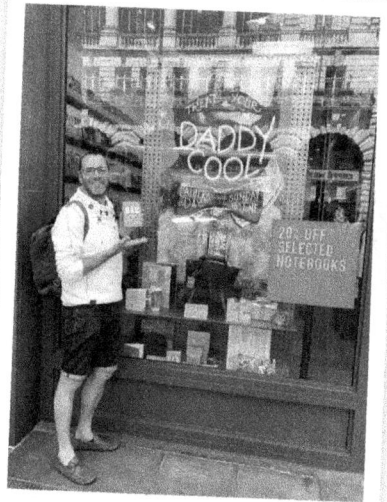

We also had the delight of having our own personal tour guide for the day, Siegfried, one of the key Rite Journey teachers from the Antwerp TRJ school KA Merksem. He offered to travel down and show us around his old home town.

Ghent is a fascinating, gorgeous, ancient city filled with beautiful cathedrals and an imposing castle within its city walls. Viewing objects of torture, knight's weapons and being in a building constructed in 1180 was simply awesome. Phoenix and I chatted about how being immersed in such history can put things in perspective.

Finally we found ourselves back at the market square and I bought myself a well-deserved Belgian Beer and Phoenix and I had a chat about alcohol. Siegfried was explaining to us that in Belgium the drinking age is 16. (Phoenix was a little deflated that he was only 9 months off being able to share a beer with me!) We chatted about different types of alcohol, responsible drinking and his feelings about it. I shared some of my experiences and it was an amazing place to have the chat, in the world's beer capital.

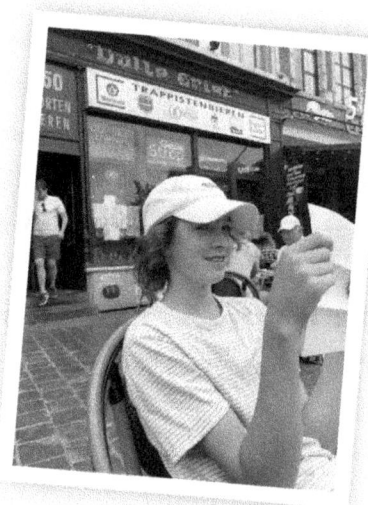

Phoenix also received 4 more letters, from friends of the family who have known him since he was a toddler. Again he has reflected on each of them, noted which qualities he admires in each of the men and written down the key ideas he gained from their communication.

The weather here has been delightful and we have loved our 2 nights living in the captain's quarters on a boat moored on the river that flows through Ghent. As we head to bed we look forward to a journey to a new European city tomorrow.

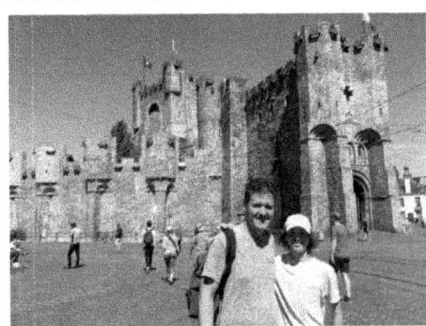

Phonix with our tour guide
Siegfried in Ghent

PART 9

Following our days in Ghent we drove north through to Amsterdam. But firstly, I wanted to share a bit of background about our time away.

This trip of Phoenix's came about courtesy of a stash of Frequent Flyer points I had hoarded. Initially we were travelling just to Europe, but I stumbled across a Frequent Flyer article which noted that a good use of points was to pay another 20,000 points and this got a 'round the world' fare which enables the traveller to stop at 5 destinations. So I approached Phoenix and asked him if he was interested in choosing 5 cities/destinations to visit and he was keen so that is how we came to be where we are.

As for Amsterdam, I had 3 major plans for conversations/experiences here. Firstly, we were catching up with dear friends from Perth, in fact the couple that I boarded with when I was 17/18.

During our visit with Gaye and Paul it was a great chance for me to chat with both Paul and Phoenix about how important Paul's presence was

in my life at that age. Paul represented a different way of being a man to my father and I realised that having a variety of different men as role models in my life was important. It was great to have the opportunity to let Phoenix know the qualities I see in Paul and also to have the chance to say thanks to Paul, in front of Phoenix. It was a lovely moment.

The second experience was choosing to visit Body Worlds, Gunther von Hagens' museum of dissected human bodies that have been preserved through the process of plastination. As we wandered through this fascinating museum I went through the **Body Stuff Suit** of the **Man Made Cards**.

The museum was amazing and what I loved was its focus on happiness. If you check out the photos you will see that there is a theme of 'what is really important in life' and it was a great way of complementing the physical body exhibition.

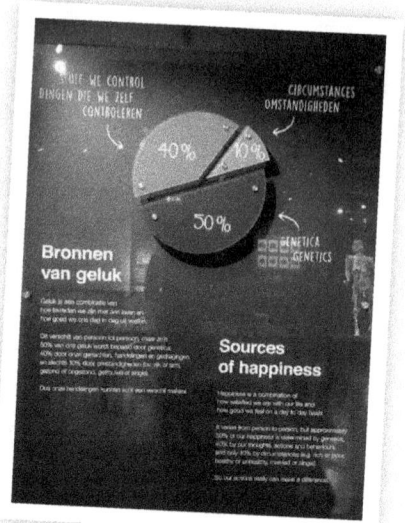

Body Worlds, Gunther von Hagens' museum of dissected human bodies

Lastly, I chose Amsterdam to be the city in which I would have the conversations with Phoenix about relationships, sex and porn. Over the course of the 3 days we chatted through the **Relationship Stuff Suit** of the **Man Made Cards**. We chatted about crushes, the stages of love, sexual orientation, gender, sex, marriage and pressures that females and males experience.

As well as chatting with Phoenix about respectful sexuality I wanted to chat about how not everyone sees sex in the same way. And so we had a tour of the red light district and learned about prostitution and its history, we chatted about how some people see sex as a purely physical act, we talked about pornography, masturbation, the differences between real sex and porn sex, the myths of porn and also the effects of excess viewing of porn. We chatted about contraception, when is the 'right time' to have sex with someone and how you might want that to be, etc.

Our tour of the red light district

Clearly such conversations can be confronting and I often hear parents concerned that in chatting to their children about such things they may be 'introducing' them to concepts too early.

Through my work I know that pretty much 100% of 14 yo boys have viewed porn and that they are probably chatting about a lot of this stuff in the schoolyard. I believe that if a caring, loving adult takes the time to explore the above topics with their boy and listens to them and their concerns, this is the best opportunity we can offer our kids.

All the way through these conversations Phoenix was interested, responsive, candid and respectful. The **Man Made Cards** were a brilliant resource to facilitate many of these conversations.

As you can see below, the front side of each card has an introductory question and then overleaf are further questions that delve a little deeper into the topic.

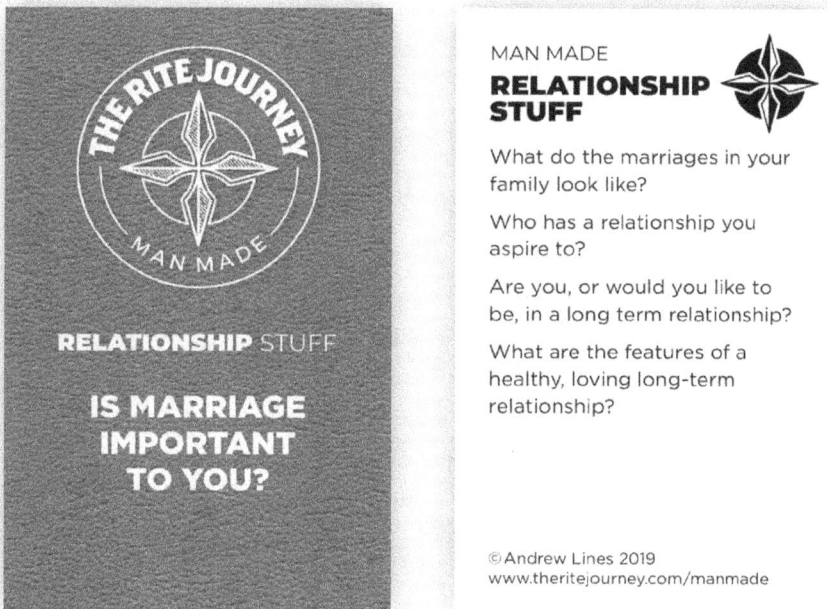

If you'd like to grab a set of the cards you can check them out **here**.

In other moments throughout the 3 days, we chatted about all sorts of things, saw how windmills work, checked out how clogs are made, ate cheese, bought some nice clothes and had a ball.

Today we have made our way back to Belgium, to Antwerp, to visit our Belgian TRJ school and the amazing teachers. It was a wonderful opportunity for Phoenix to hang out with Siegfried's twin boys. We chatted about the importance of finding good role models but also being a good role model to younger people. Tomorrow, we'll be moving on again.

PART 10

I firmly believe that when we approach experiences and offer ourselves with a heart-full intent all sorts of other things 'move' and occur as a part of that generous, whole-hearted gesture.

It's a bit like Goethe's quote about commitment:

"Until one is committed, there is hesitancy, the chance to draw back, always ineffectiveness. Concerning all acts of initiative (and creation), there is one elementary truth the ignorance of which kills countless ideas and splendid plans: that the moment one definitely commits oneself, then Providence moves too. All sorts of things occur to help one that would never otherwise have occurred. A whole stream of events issues from the decision, raising in one's favor all manner of unforeseen incidents and meetings and material assistance, which no man could have dreamed would have come his way. Whatever you can do, or dream you can do, begin it. Boldness has genius, power, and magic in it. Begin it now."

Anyway, I believe Phoenix and I had one of those experiences today. We had a brief 6 hour stopover in London and instead of hanging out at the airport we caught the express train to London.

And guess who we saw???

The Queen!

It was 'Trooping the Colours' and we saw all manner of things. Phoenix could not believe it!

I love noticing when these gifts in life occur... and have today encouraged Phoenix to keep an eye out for these moments in his life too... and to be grateful for them.

PART 11

It is now two weeks since we saw the Queen in London.

Since then Phoenix has been joined by his older sister (17yo) Danté and we have travelled to Norway, Sweden, Ireland, England and Italy. It has been a lovely opportunity for us to travel and spend quality time together.

Some of the significant moments of the last two weeks with Phoenix and Dante have been their contribution at the wedding blessing ceremony for me and my wife Becky, a visit to Stratford Upon Avon, some intentional reflective conversations with the three of us and an adventure to The Matterhorn.

Wedding Blessing – We were in Leicester to offer my wife, Becky's, UK family and friends the opportunity to celebrate our marriage which was in Australia in December.

As we didn't have the minister with us to repeat our vows, I asked Phoenix and Danté if they would be happy to be the ones who presented the blessing and the vows and they both agreed. It was such an honour to have them both speak the words that were spoken at our Aussie wedding. And we couldn't believe how brave it was for them to do this in front of the UK crew.

Stratford Upon Avon - We visited Shakespeare's birthplace and chatted about his legacy and my love of his work as an English teacher.

Italy Conversation - as we spent time around Venice, Verona, Lake Iseo and walking around Monte Isola, we chatted about love and relationships, including the female perspective which Danté could provide.

We visited Verona, original inspiration for Shakespeare's Romeo and Juliet, and found Juliet's balcony and the brass statue (which legend says if you touch her right breast you will be lucky in love!) These experiences led to conversations with Danté and Phoenix. I asked Danté to share with her brother her responses to these questions:

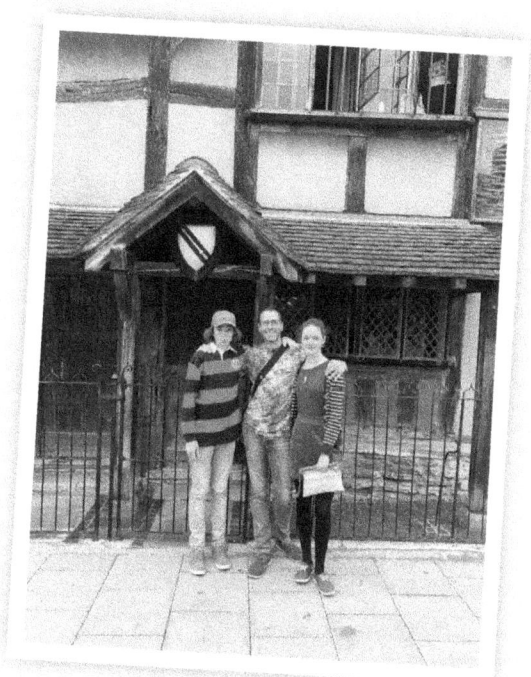

Our visit to Shakespeare's birthplace

What do you wish males knew about how it is being a female?

What do you wish young men/males did more of?

What do you wish young men/males did less of?

What do you love about being female?

What do you find challenging about being female?

This led to some insightful conversations for Phoenix to hear, from a female perspective. I believe that it's important for our boys and young men to hear these opinions from females in their lives as it helps build empathy.

The Matterhorn - From Italy we moved on to Switzerland and had the amazing opportunity to travel on one of the world's steepest trains to see The Matterhorn.

Both Phoenix and I are transfixed by mountains and so this was the chance of a lifetime, but it was very expensive.

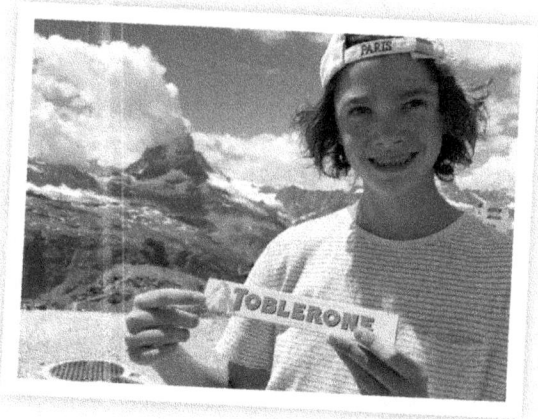

I took this opportunity to chat with Phoenix about my choice to spend money on experiences rather than 'things'. We chatted about the fact that some people choose to amass material possessions and that others choose to collect experiences.

We are currently in La Tzoumaz in the Swiss Alps where yesterday we reached the summit of another mountain, Mont Fort. However right now, Phoenix is preparing for his solo experience tonight!

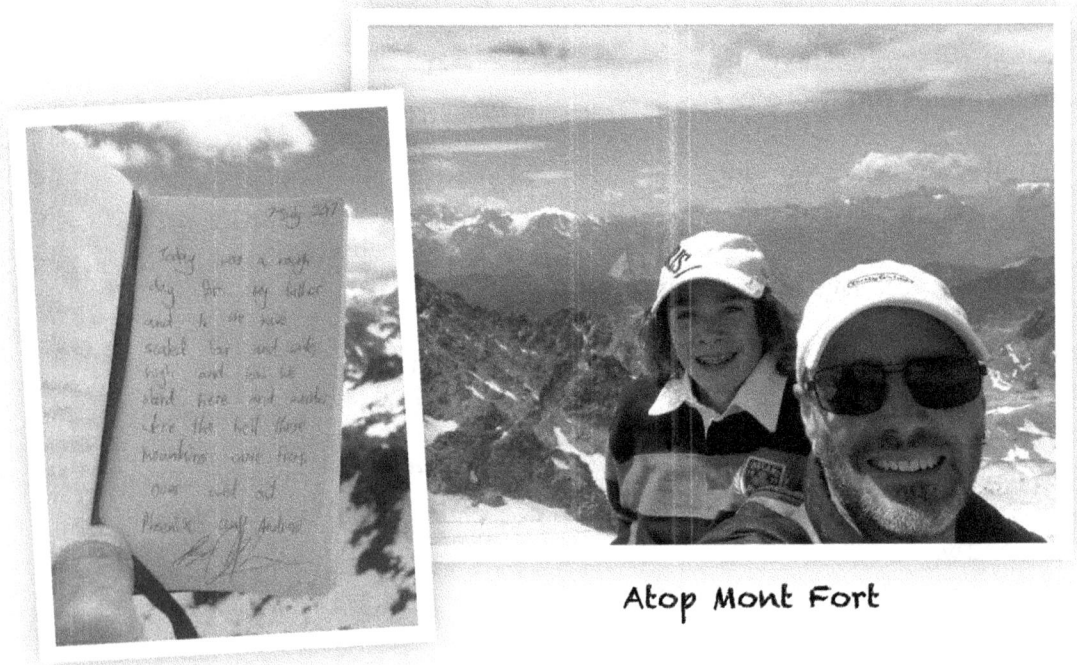

Atop Mont Fort

PART 12

Last night was one of Phoenix's major challenges for his journey. His solo night out in the Swiss Alps. In the afternoon Phoenix set off for 24 hours alone with his quilt, a pocket knife and a bottle of water. No phone, no food, no book, nothing to take him away from his own self and thoughts. It was a technology free time, a time of fasting, a time of silence and a time of reflection. His main task was to spend time with himself and to create a nature totem in gratitude for that space offering him that experience.

This morning Phoenix reflected on his poor night's sleep ("How are you meant to sleep on a 90 degree slope???"). He noticed how hungry he was (in typical teenage boy fashion). He reflected on how easily he coped without his phone and how much he enjoyed whittling wood with his pocket knife. His nature totem included symbolism of the gentleness and beauty of nature, of the harshness of nature and of the impact of humans on nature.

I highly recommend a 24 hour solo for every teenager. Our Rite Journey schools offer the process for their students as one of their major challenges.

PART 13

Some of you may remember one of the early posts from Phoenix's Journey in NYC where we walked into a Fed Ex Express store to do some printing and saw that they had 2 books for sale (in the entire store). One was 'The Places You'll Go' by Dr Seuss which I bought for Phoenix. The other was 'Primary Greatness' by Stephen Covey which I bought for myself or at least I thought.

Today I had some downtime, a month on from the purchase, and I flicked open the book to the foreword and read the below words! I immediately found Phoenix and read them to him. How relevant they are for Phoenix's Journey to Manhood. Aim for Primary Greatness rather than Secondary Greatness.

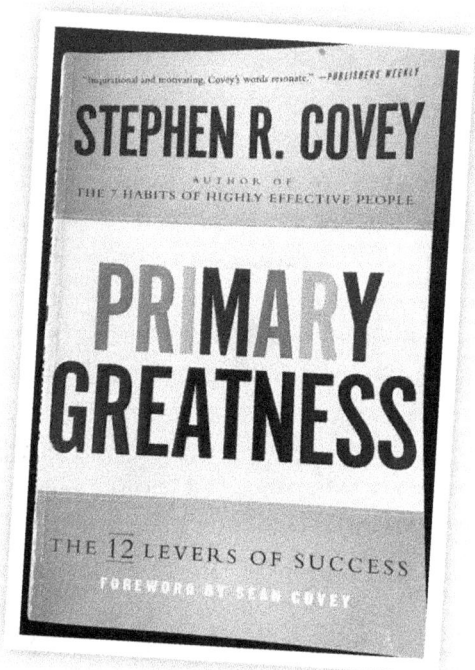

He was a great teacher, first by his example, and then by his words, and I was deeply influenced by his insights. One of the fundamental things he continually taught me is that there are two ways to live: a life of primary greatness or a life of secondary greatness. Primary greatness is who you really are—your character, your integrity, your deepest motives and desires. Secondary greatness is popularity, title, position, fame, fortune, and honors. He taught me not to worry about secondary greatness and to focus on primary greatness. He also noted that secondary greatness would often—but not always—follow those who achieve primary greatness, and that primary greatness had its own intrinsic rewards, such as peace of mind, contribution, and rich and rewarding relationships. These rewards far outweigh the extrinsic rewards of secondary greatness—money, popularity, and the self-absorbed, pleasure-ridden life that we too often consider "success."

This book is a collection of several of my father's best essays that have never appeared in book form before and aren't well known. But

PART 14

We continue **The Challenges** stage of Phoenix's journey which started with his solo experience in the Swiss Alps.

During this phase he will have a series of challenges, some will be physical, others mental... some will be easier, some harder, some individual, some with his sister, some shorter, some longer.

I won't mention all of his challenges here (there have already been a number in the previous 4 weeks - I will detail them later) but today he successfully completed 2 of them

1. To learn the phonetic alphabet.

2. To navigate his way (for himself and his sister) from our accommodation in La Marais, Paris to the Louvre and then to find his way through the Louvre to the Mona Lisa and to send me a photo of himself in front of it. He managed both of them successfully!

Tomorrow he will have another major challenge which I have been preparing him for since the start of our trip. His MYSTERY challenge.

He knows it will be at the Eiffel Tower...and he has been worrying about it for most of the trip! I have given him no other info about this challenge but he was told tonight to eat well before bed, drink plenty of liquids and to get a good sleep!

Phonetic Alphabet

Alpha	November
Bravo	Oscar
Charlie	Papa
Delta	Quebec
Echo	Romeo
Foxtrot	Sierra
Golf	Tango
Hotel	Uniform
India	Victor
Juliet	Whiskey
Kilo	Xray
Lima	Yankee
Mike	Zulu

Phoenix completing his challenge at the Mona Lisa

PART 15

Over the past week we have been building up to Phoenix's Mystery Challenge. He knew it would be happening at the Eiffel Tower. He knew he would receive no details at all about it. He knew it would start at around 4pm and be finished by 7pm. He had asked plenty of questions about the challenge in the lead up and it was clear it had been weighing on his mind for the preceding weeks and especially for the duration of today. He had ideas as to what it would be and I had some fun playing on those...

The challenge was built up over the weeks leading up to it with the intention of actually creating a level of worry, to cause the 'initiate' to begin to write stories in their mind. The greater the worry - the greater the lesson!

Finally the challenge time arrives and Phoenix nervously awaits the instruction. In the video I took of Phoenix as I explained his Mystery Challenge you can see his nervous fidgeting and then some disbelief/relief when he hears what the actual task is.

The beauty of the mystery challenge is the conversation afterwards, the illumination on how as humans, when there is an unknown on the horizon, we worry and write stories. Generally we write worst case scenarios.

Phoenix being told about his mystery challenge and worried that it would be horrific!

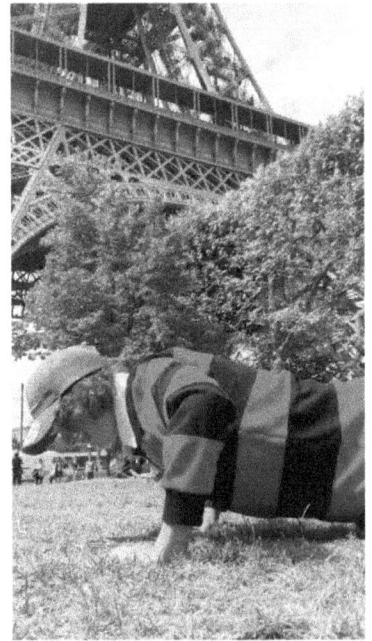

Phoenix doing his mystery challenge (One push up!)

Phoenix and I discussed the 'stories' he had written about the challenge, how heavily it had weighed on his mind and that worry is a choice. We can also choose not to worry, perhaps rather to wonder. We explored how worry is mostly about things we can't control and can't change and how our body's physiological response to worry, to our thoughts, is almost identical as if that imagined situation was actually happening. We noted that our bodies aren't made to worry for hours at a time, that rather we have a 'fight or flight' response which is designed to be engaged for a matter of seconds. Worry, however, puts our bodies in this state for hours and that leads to physical and mental dis-ease.

I shared with Phoenix how understanding this concept changed my life and that reading Eckhart Tolle's 'The Power of Now' was a major transformative moment for me. We discussed how we can observe our thinking and notice when we 'fall into' worry and then we have a choice to fix that and to think differently.

The mystery challenge is a very real experience of exactly this and one that all teens could have to help them understand the issue of worry.

Phoenix has now been given his final 3 challenges... to see out our time in London.

1. 24 hours without his phone! (We are 16 hours in!)
2. 7 random acts of kindness (He will tell us 4 of them and keep 3 of them to himself.)
3. Learn to knit (being taught by his sister in a London Pub)

Phoenix learning how to knit

His challenge program is almost complete.

"Lo and behold, it turns out that 85% of what subjects worried about never happened, and with the 15% that did happen, 79% of subjects discovered either they could handle the difficulty better than expected, or the difficulty taught them a lesson worth learning. This means that 97% of what you worry over is not much more than a fearful mind punishing you with exaggerations and misperceptions."
(http://m.huffpost.com/us/entry/8028368)

PART 16

Here's a recap of **The Challenges** element of Phoenix's Journey.
The Challenges are one of the 7 steps of The Rite Journey:

1. The Calling
2. The Departure
3. The Following
4. The Challenges
5. The Abyss
6. The Return
7. The Homecoming

THE CALLING   THE DEPARTURE   THE FOLLOWING

THE CHALLENGES   THE ABYSS   THE RETURN   THE HOMECOMING

I decided upon 7 Challenges for Phoenix over
the past week, involving a variety of types of tasks.

They were:

1. Navigation Challenge - to find his way through Paris to the Louvre and then through the Louvre to find the Mona Lisa
2. Learn the phonetic alphabet
3. 24 hours without his phone
4. Knitting - learn to knit and knit a scarf
5. 7 Random Acts of Kindness - 4 which he would share with me and 3 that he would keep to himself.
6. Solo – a night out in the Swiss Alps, fasting, with only a quilt, some water and a pocket knife.
7. Mystery challenge - an easy challenge which is not mentioned, but built up over time to create worry. Phoenix's challenge was at The Eiffel Tower - he imagined it would involve climbing or jumping or abseiling etc but it actually was just one push up.

The aim of the Challenge Program (which is also implemented in our Rite Journey schools) is to help Phoenix understand that life will always present challenges and difficulties, along with the lesson that failure is ok, and in fact a better teacher than success.

There is one final challenge that you (and Phoenix will hear about in the next day or so... it is a part of The Return and will be one of the culminating moments of his journey.

PART 17

As Phoenix's journey comes to an end we begin to reflect on the themes that we have covered over the last 5 weeks and look forward to the years ahead.

Tonight we went to see The Lion King and it was the perfect performance to see to explore Phoenix's journey and move into manhood.

For those of you familiar with the story you will remember that it is about Mufasa, the father, and Simba, the son.

Simba needs to ultimately come to terms with the death of his father and taking on his own responsibility in life rather than simply enjoying the good life in the jungle with Pumbaa and Timon.

He also learns lessons about choosing not to worry, who can forget Hakuna Matata, and embracing the influence of his ancestors.

Mufasa: Simba, let me tell you something that my father told me. Look at the stars. The great Kings of the past who are connected to us and look down on us look from those stars.

Simba: Really?

Mufasa: Yes. So whenever you feel alone, just remember that those Kings will always be there to guide you... and so will I.

What a serendipitous piece of theatre to see with Phoenix.

Our discussion afterwards covered each of the above themes and along with this I also chatted about 3 shifts from child psychology to adult psychology which seemed to fit perfectly.

Child: Life is about me and what I can get
Adult: Life is about others and what I can give

Child: Life is easy
Adult: Life is hard

Child: I'll live forever
Adult: I am going to die

We talked about service to others and Phoenix's random acts of kindness.

We reflected on his challenges acknowledging that life is hard.

We chatted about mortality and the fact that more probably than not, one day I will die and Phoenix will still be around. But that my spirit will live on in him as will the spirit of his grandfathers, as does the spirit of his great grandfathers etc.

We also had a conversation reflecting on the fact that one day Phoenix will also die.

The Lion King was just amazing, Becky, myself and the 3 kids absolutely loved it.

And again, as has happened many times on this journey, serendipity stepped in. Upon walking into that performance I had no idea it would be the perfect story to share with Phoenix in the closing days of his journey.

PART 18

Well, our journey is coming to an end.

A couple of final parts of the process have been completed in our hotel room at Heathrow Airport as we begin our travels home. These moments mark **The Return** part of Phoenix's journey.

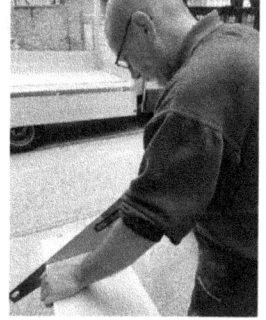

The first was a board breaking. This symbolised Phoenix's crossing over the threshold from boy to young man.

I had managed to find a timber shop nearby to Hammersmith, where we were staying, in London. It happened to be open on a Saturday morning and a kind gentleman hand sawed Phoenix's board!

On his board Phoenix wrote something that symbolised, for him, the boy to man transition as well as adding the symbol that he created for himself 6 weeks ago. At our hotel room we went through the symbolism of breaking the board and also some visualisation processes to assist in that.

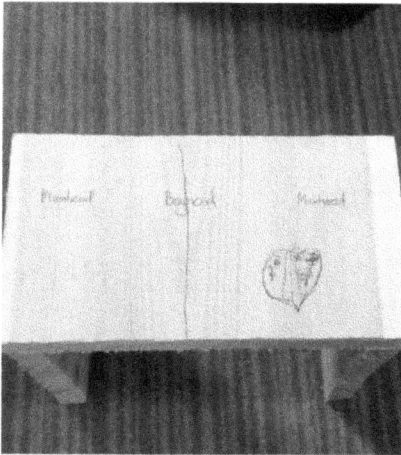

Phoenix's board for breaking.

Phoenix wasn't convinced that he could break the board. And Interestingly on his first attempt he didn't break it.

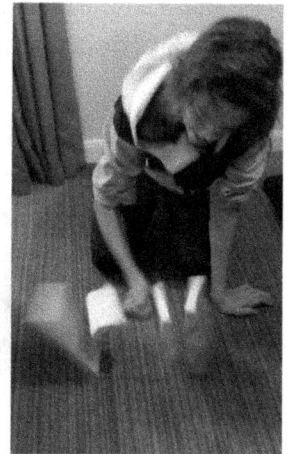

After we had a bit more of a chat he gave it a second go!

Finally I presented Phoenix with a symbol representing his journey.

A compass key ring which represents the importance of the journey over the destination but also the importance of his internal compass which will help keep him on track throughout the rest of his life.

The symbolism of a key ring also represents the massive freedom he will feel in 6 months when he is legally able to get his learner's permit for driving but also equally, the responsibility that comes with being a driver.

It is no different from becoming a man, there is a balance between both freedom and responsibility which I'm hoping Phoenix is beginning to understand from his journey.

We also discussed the lessons he had learned over his journey and he documented those that stood out for him in his journal.

Now we have a few days in Tokyo prior to returning home.

And upon our return we will complete Phoenix's journey process with **The Homecoming**. And you'll find out about that in a week or two!

PART 19

The final stage of The Rite Journey is **The Homecoming**. This is the moment where Phoenix meets back up in his community/family and is honoured but also commits to returning as a young man (not a boy) and presents a vision of who he'd like to be as a man.

We invited the family who were present at **The Departure** and his task was to provide the meal for everyone, present a powerpoint that outlined his journey, share the significant lessons he had learned on his journey, and commit to stepping up into his role as a young man.

It was a beautiful afternoon of celebrating and honouring Phoenix and his transition from boy to man. And now it is up to us to expect him to act as a young man... and it is up to him to step into his new role.

(If there was something I would have done differently with Phoenix's Homecoming, I'd have also invited each of the mentors who had written letters to Phoenix along to the celebration. I would have had Phoenix buy a small gift for each of them while we were away and at The Homecoming I would have loved for him to have shared with each of those mentors the lesson he had learned from their letter and the quality that he sees in them that he would like to replicate.)

His next significant moment will be his **Release Ceremony** when he turns 18!

AFTERWORD – March 2020

The final Rite of Passage of childhood I call **The Release**. This process occurs on an individual's 18th birthday and acknowledges their step into independent adulthood and our 'step back' as parents. It is an intentional moment in which we acknowledge to our 18 year old that they are now an adult and legally have the same place as us, their parents.

To celebrate his birthday we gathered together with family and friends and I let Phoenix know that I will be making a conscious effort from now on to enable him to develop into his own person, that I won't choose to force my opinions or thoughts onto him any longer but, of course, will always be there for him should he like to seek out my opinion or advice.

It is an empowering gesture intending to provide him with space to grow rather than restricting him or causing him to be overly worried about pleasing me.

I let him know that a part of life is making mistakes and failing and that I will always be there to support him, but will not be preventing his learning by rescuing him.

(The process is also a choice for me to own 'my stuff' as a parent and not to burden my children with it.)

As well as this public recognition there is also a token of the moment which I suggest is given on the 18th birthday.

For Phoenix I chose to give him a hip-flask with the engraving "With Freedom Comes Responsibility", which reiterates the message he received on his journey years earlier.

A final element of **The Release** process with Phoenix is to attend a counselling session together in which I ask him to share with me any issues he's had with my fathering over the years.

I want him to tell me when he's felt unsupported, let down, ignored etc. I want him to have the opportunity to clear the air with me simply reflectively listening to him.

It is a difficult process but one that I feel releases any ongoing resentments or 'skeletons in the closet' that might exist between us. It feels like a cleansing and is intended to clear the path for my ongoing relationship with him, in its new incarnation, as two adults.

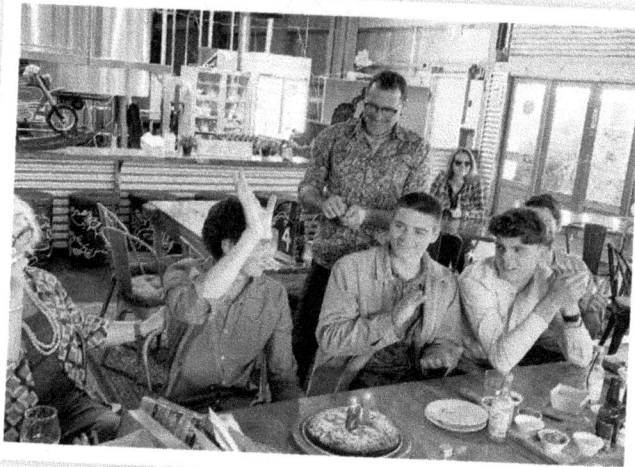

If you would like more information on creating a similar **Rite Journey - Man Made** for the boy in your life please email me: **andrew@theritejourney.com**

The Man Made Conversation Cards are available at:
www.theritejourney.com/manmade

www.ingramcontent.com/pod-product-compliance
Lightning Source LLC
Chambersburg PA
CBHW080552030426
42337CB00024B/4849